TRADITIONS AND CELEB

DIWALI

by Anita Nahta Amin

PEBBLE
a capstone imprint

Pebble Explore is published by Pebble, an imprint of Capstone.
1710 Roe Crest Drive
North Mankato, Minnesota 56003
capstonepub.com

Library of Congress Cataloging-in-Publication Data
Names: Amin, Anita Nahta, author.
Title: Diwali / Anita Nahta Amin.
Description: North Mankato, Minnesota : Pebble, [2022] | Series: Traditions & celebrations | Includes bibliographical references and index. | Audience: Ages 5-8 | Audience: Grades K-1 | Summary: "Diwali is about celebrating! It honors the Hindu story of Rama. Sikhs, Buddhists, and Jains also celebrate Diwali. To celebrate this Festival of Lights, people light lamps, watch fireworks, and dance. Others might exchange cards and presents. Readers will discover how a shared holiday can have multiple traditions and be celebrated in all sorts of ways"— Provided by publisher.
Identifiers: LCCN 2021012685 (print) | LCCN 2021012686 (ebook) | ISBN 9781663908315 (hardcover) | ISBN 9781663920898 (paperback) | ISBN 9781663908285 (pdf) | ISBN 9781663908308 (kindle edition)
Subjects: LCSH: Divali—Juvenile literature.
Classification: LCC BL1239.82.D58 A48 2022 (print) | LCC BL1239.82.D58 (ebook) | DDC 394.265/45—dc23
LC record available at https://lccn.loc.gov/2021012685
LC ebook record available at https://lccn.loc.gov/2021012686

Image Credits
Alamy: Christian Hütter, 16, Indiapicture, 20, Morten Svenningsen, 11; Getty Images: danilovi, 9; Newscom: Hindustan Times, 25, Reuters/RANU ABHELAKH, 28, Sipa USA/Pacific Press, 5, Sipa/SOPA Images/Avijit Ghosh, 1, 26, ZUMA Press/Narayan Maharjan, 29; Shutterstock: Creative Minds2, 23, CRS PHOTO, 12, Davide Gandolfi, 27, Image bug, 13, JOAT, Cover, Joshua Gao, 8, Nitish Waila, 19, Sabrina Bracher, 6, Snehal Jeevan Pailkar, 14, szefei, 15

Artistic elements: Shutterstock: Rafal Kulik

Editorial Credits
Editor: Erika L. Shores; Designer: Dina Her; Media Researcher: Jo Miller; Production Specialist: Tori Abraham

All internet sites appearing in back matter were available and accurate when this book was sent to press.

TABLE OF CONTENTS

Words in **bold** are in the glossary.

WHAT IS DIWALI?

Whiz! Bang! Pop! Fireworks burst across the night sky. All over India, small oil lamps light up the darkness. They glow in homes and shops. Neighbors give each other sweets as gifts. Nut fudge! Sweet milk patties! Bean balls!

It is a time of joy. It is Diwali. It is the Festival of Lights. Some people call it Deepavali. This means "row of lights" in Sanskrit. This Indian language is the oldest in the world.

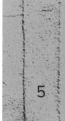

A Hindu mother and child
celebrate Diwali.

More than 1 billion people in the world celebrate Diwali. In India, it is a big holiday. People of most faiths, or **religions**, join in the fun.

Some **Hindus** honor a holy king during Diwali. Some honor gods and goddesses. Hindu myths are stories from long ago. These myths said gods and goddesses destroyed evil beings.

Diwali can last for five days. The holiday reminds people that good is stronger than evil.

For people who are **Sikhs**, Diwali honors a **guru**. He was a teacher who was freed from a bad leader long ago.

Jains and **Buddhists** celebrate too. They honor the teachers who started their religions.

Sikhs celebrate Diwali.

A Buddhist temple during Diwali

WHEN IS DIWALI?

The main day of Diwali is on the fifteenth day of the Hindu month, Kartik. No moon shines that night. It is the darkest night of the month. It is also the Hindu New Year.

The Hindu calendar is lunar. It is based on the moon. Most people in the world use the solar calendar. Solar has to do with the sun.

Solar and lunar dates don't always match. On the solar calendar, Diwali dates change each year. The holiday can fall in October or November.

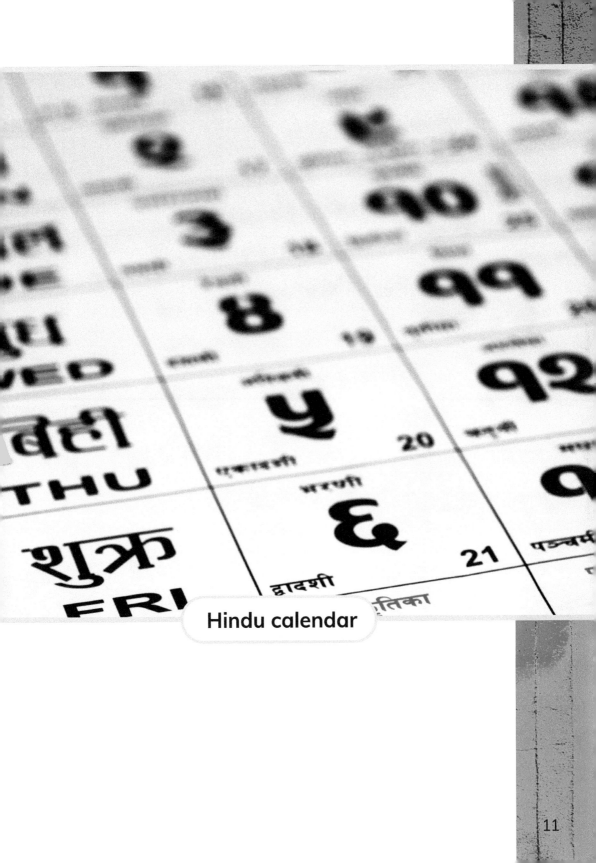

Hindu calendar

FIVE DAYS OF FUN

DAY 1

Sweep the floors. Wipe the walls. Clean the cupboards. On the first day of Diwali, people clean their homes, offices, and temples.

People make **rangoli** art. Colored sand is spread on the floor. People might use flowers or rice instead. The sand, flowers, or rice are made into shapes, such as flowers or birds.

rangoli art

Lakshmi statue

Garlands are hung around doors. The garlands are strings of flowers and mango leaves.

People hope **Lakshmi** will see their clean, pretty places. She is the Hindu goddess of good luck and wealth. People pray that she will bless them.

The first day is also a big shopping day. People buy gold. They buy cooking tools. They buy clothes and gifts.

Diyas are lit at night. They are set out to light up the darkest night. The diya is a symbol. A person's inner light is stronger than the darkness of evil. Diyas welcome Lakshmi too.

Some people light diyas to honor **Rama**. A Hindu myth says a demon, or evil **spirit**, made Rama leave his lands. Years later, Rama destroyed the demon. People lit diyas to welcome him back.

A family picks out treats at a shop in India.

DAY 2

In parts of southern India, day two is the main day. But for most people, it is like Diwali Eve. It is called Little Diwali.

The day starts with a holy bath. Everyone in a household gets one. They say it cleans away evil. Later, people pray for dead loved ones.

Then everyone gets ready for guests. They cook or buy sweets. Family and friends visit each other.

DAY 3

It is Diwali Day! It is time for fun, feasts, and fireworks. People dress up in fancy clothes. They go to parties. They give gifts to loved ones. The gifts are sweets, coins, or gold.

Diyas, fireworks, and sparklers light up the night. People pray at temples. They pray that Lakshmi will bless them. They play card games. People of many faiths celebrate.

The Golden Temple
in India

DAY 4

The new year starts on the fourth day. Shop owners pray for a year of good sales. They start a new book called a ledger. It keeps track of what the owner has bought and sold.

Husbands and wives honor their love. The wife prays for her husband's good health. Then he gives her gifts.

DAY 5

The last day is for siblings. Brothers visit their sisters. They honor their love. A sister prays for her brother's good health. She dots red paste and dry rice on his forehead. This is for good luck.

A brother gives his sister gifts. He promises to take care of her. Then they will eat a meal together.

OTHER CUSTOMS

There are many ways to take part in Diwali. Some towns in India give thanks for a good harvest. They pray for good luck with their cattle, money, and rice or other grains.

In a town in western India, children build lamps out of sticks. They go door-to-door. They sing songs. People give them oil and grain.

A cow is fed as part
of a Diwali celebration.

One state in India celebrates a month after the others. This state was said to be far from Rama's lands. It took a month longer to hear about his return. A battle in a Hindu myth started on this day too. Some people honor this battle. Here, Diwali is three days long.

A city on the Ganges River has an important day called Dev Diwali. This day honors gods. It is held 15 days after Diwali. People light 1.5 million diyas! They line the steps going down to the river.

People around the world take part in Diwali. Some places in the world honor all five days. Some have a shorter holiday.

A woman dressed as Lakshmi leads a celebration in the country of Suriname.

Some places have big parties. Others celebrate quietly. In U.S. cities, like New York City, people give concerts during Diwali. In the country of Nepal, the holiday is called Tihar. Dogs, crows, cows, and oxen are blessed. They get treats and flowers.

There are many ways to celebrate Diwali. In the end, the holiday is about one thing. Good always wins against evil. *Shubh Diwali!* Happy Diwali!

GLOSSARY

Buddhist (BOO-dist)—a person who follows the religion of Buddhism; Buddhism is based on the teachings of Buddha

diya (DEE-ah)—a small clay bowl filled with oil and a wick to be lit

guru (GOO-roo)—a Sanskrit word that means teacher; a teacher of Indian religion

Hindu (HIN-doo)—a person who practices the religion of Hinduism; Hindus believe that they must live in harmony with universal laws

Jain (JAYN)—a person who follows the ancient Indian religion of Jainism

Lakshmi (LAAK-shmee)—a Hindu goddess of wealth and good luck

Rama (RAH-mah)—an ancient Hindu king and god according to legends

rangoli (raang-GOW-lee)—an art pattern, often of nature, made with colored sand, rice, or flowers

religion (ri-LIJ-uhn)—a set of spiritual beliefs that people follow

Sikh (SEEK)—a person who follows the Indian religion of Sikhism

spirit (SPIHR-it)—another name for a ghost

READ MORE

Mattern, Joanne. *India*. Minneapolis: Jump!, 2019.

Sferazza, Jeff. *Holidays Around the World*. New York: Gareth Stevens Publishing, 2019.

Soundararajan, Chitra. *Let's Look at India*. North Mankato, MN: Capstone Press, 2020.

INTERNET SITES

Diwali Facts for Kids
kids.kiddle.co/Diwali

Diwali: Festival of Lights
kids.nationalgeographic.com/explore/diwali/

India for Kids
kids-world-travel-guide.com/india-for-kids.html

INDEX